Bourne Bridge

Bourne Bridge

Poems ~ Alice Kociemba

Alice Kociemba

Turning Point

Published by Turning Point
P.O. Box 541106
Cincinnati, OH 45254-1106

ISBN: 9781625491749

Poetry Editor: Kevin Walzer
Business Editor: Lori Jareo

Visit us on the web at
www.turningpointbooks.com

Acknowledgments

Grateful acknowledgment is made to the following publications in which some of these poems first appeared, some in earlier versions:

Atlanta Review, International Publication Award, "Paper Route"

Atlanta Review, International Merit Award, "Death of Teaticket Hardware"

The Aurorean, "beneath this bridge," "Bourne Bridge," "Cape Cod Fog," "Meditation in the Garden," "Snug Cottage," "Wetlands in November"

Avocet, "Diva," "Labor Day," "Autumnal Equinox"

Cape Cod Poetry Review, "Snapshots of Sippewissett Marsh"

Comstock Review, "Self-Portrait"

International Psychoanalysis, "That dream of you again"

Main Street Rag, "If I wake up dead," "A Brief Stint as a Nurse's Aide at Sunnyside Manor"

Off the Coast, "After the Funeral"

Plainsongs, "Before Dreaming," "Wetlands in October"

Roanoke Review, "Willie Nelson, 4 a.m."

Salamander, "Betrayals," "Mind's Eye"

Slant, "Kitchen Sky"

Appreciation

To the Jamaica Pond Poets—Dorothy Derifield, Carolyn Gregory, Holly Guran, Audrey Henderson, Susanna Kittredge, Dorian Kotsiopoulos, Jim LaFond-Lewis, Jennifer Markell, Sybille Rex, Alan Smith, Sandra Storey and Gary Whited; these poems would not be ready for the world without your insight and encouragement.

To my poetry teachers, Eva Bourke, Mark Doty, Robert Pinsky and Daniel Tobin, thank you for teaching craft with compassion. And especially to Fred Marchant, whose teaching and mentoring has made an enormous impact, not just on my writing, but also in my life.

Special gratitude to the West Falmouth Library and Pamela T. Olson for embracing the *Calliope Poetry Series*, and to all its featured poets, special event readers, Mark Doty and Jorie Graham, Winter Craft Workshop instructors and our open mic poets.

Thanks to the Poetry Discussion Group at the Falmouth Public Library and Mass Poetry's Common Threads project, which has sustained my enthusiasm for reading and discussing contemporary poets.

And to *Falmouth Reads Together* for selecting Robert Pinsky's *Favorite Poems Project* and to Robert, especially, for his steadfast commitment to expanding the audience for poetry.

To my dear poet-friends, Dorothy Derifield and Susan Donnelly, I can't imagine this book without your good heads and hearts in it. Deepest appreciation to

Martha's Vineyard artist Genevieve Jacobs, whose collage cover art evokes the essence of crossing over the Bourne Bridge.

For the fine editorial eyes of Katy Sternberger, for the graphic design expertise of Terri Hare, for the artistic flair of Kathleen Casey, and for the steadfast support of Rich Youmans...there is no other word but *thanks*!

Gratitude beyond words for the friendship and love of my son, David Kociemba — to whom this book is dedicated.

Table of Contents

marrow

stone

marsh

beneath this bridge
　　　　barnacles cling
to summer

marrow

Paper Route
(for Tom)

Ogallala, Nebraska. Population 25
or so it seemed. At quarter till dawn,
he biked to the station before it was demolished
by the engineer's "speed and negligence."
Drunk, no doubt, when the 5:40
heading west to North Platte derailed.
We made the Evening News even in Lincoln.
It is still news at Ollie's Big Game Lounge —
a sure sign the end of the world is coming, soon.
Over rattlesnake pizza and Coors
men with Marlboros
take that "told you so" stance
toward strangers and newcomers.
But they are right in one respect,
no city dweller has ever seen the sky.
So still, so deep, so bright — a safety net
for those who fall upward into wonder.
You forget for a while the littleness of people.
Until the whistle breaks the night
with one long blast and two quick
volleys of civilization,
as aching a sound as he ever heard
in that dusty time of yearning.
The train brought the world to town
at least for five minutes
when the *Omaha World Herald*
plopped onto the platform, headline up.
His ticket to freedom.

Kitchen Sky

Isabelle Alice and her china sailed the North Atlantic
from Dundee to Boston, without a chip.
Passed down from mother to daughter to daughter,
to me, the namesake daughter,
it was always washed by hand,
an act of love
for the woman who cared so much
to carry it so far.

Each surface carefully cleaned,
as she noticed:
This one plate. This one bowl.
This one cup and saucer.
Wash   rinse   dry   set aside.
Do it again   and again   in a rhythm
that calms the hurried soul, who can't
get ahead of herself.

Did she daydream of the life left behind?
Or look up and get lost in kitchen sky:
The changing hues, first so blue,
until a magenta crack appears low
on the horizon. In a final burst of light,
the dish-colors appear, yellow on blue,
with a little spray of pink against
a tarnished silver sky.

The Watch

(for my brother, Bill Bene, 1943-1979)

He rode the buses
from Roxbury to Southie
in his Roman collar;

walked the kids in,
past the red-hot crowd,
in Celtic green and crucifixes.

Then walked back out
to listen. Fear bruised
his city.

And he read the names
of the Vietnam dead
on the Boston Common.
Blood brothers now—
their bones without color.

He wrote his own funeral
in a #2 pencil. *Choose life—*
the Old Testament reading.
The music: Sinatra's *My Way*.

Thirty years tick by and I still
hear my son's keening cry:
"I hate Huncle Bill,
give me back the flowers!"

He's now the spit of him—
the hair, the hands, the humor.
Bill taught him chess,
the Queen's Gambit.

Still I hear him say,
"How about a game
before bedtime?"

A man's watch
sits on the windowsill
glints in late day sun
as I do dishes.

I should sit awhile.
Think. Forget the chores,
watch the sun go down.

No pockets in the shroud

(for my mother, Isabelle Dimery Bene)

...she'd always say to someone
who had enough but worried anyway.
You leave this world as you come in—
not poor, but without a penny.

She taught me how to save
the remnants of a summer day.
Dishes undone, time to walk
before the setting sun.

On that pebbled shore,
we'd bend and pick specks of glass,
green, amber, rarer blue:
what the tide bequeaths you.

"Look up—a mackerel sky!
It'll rain by morning."

Now the sea glass lamp
shines like that speckled shore.
And I can hear the crash of wave,
receding into whispers.

Easy come. Easy go. Let go...

Happy Birthday

My mother told me every year
        I was an inconvenient child.

Born two days before Christmas
        and a month too soon.

She had cooked and cleaned all day
        even scrubbed the bathroom down
        for family   who seldom visited.

After all, she was the one who moved away
        to the City, where there were
        Criminals. And Catholics.
And worse, she became one.

Serves her right for getting pregnant again
at 39 with number 5. Didn't she know
        she was too old for that?

But they would come
and bring the pies and presents,
        wrapped in holier-than-thou.

They arrived promptly at one.
The roast would be done at two.
The other labor had begun at noon,

so she knew she'd be leaving before dinner.

My mother always ended her story with a smile:
"It was the best Christmas I ever had—
thanks to you. I was waited on
and didn't have to lift a finger."

My Mother's Junk Drawer

Admit it. You have at least one—
the bottom drawer in the pantry.
Or if you're excessive, all the ones
in the old blue bureau, under the poster—
I Like Ike—cute in his khaki uniform.
There's a treasure trove of twistees,
and in another crumbling plastic bag—
elastics, also crumbling.
Dried out black Magic Markers,
some with their caps on.
Nubs of #2 pencils,
one splintered thin, the perfect wedge
for the wobbly kitchen table.
More nuts than bolts.
Red thumbtacks, a ruler.
The gray, cracked sink stopper.
A carpenter's level.
The frayed cord to the waffle iron.
Extra fuses, some burnt out,
in with the good ones.

Becoming Aunt Irene

One day you look down
spot Kleenex stuffed in the cuff
of the red cardigan, hear yourself sniffling—
those allergy pills, a dollar apiece...
Then you start ironing sheets;
wrinkles disturb your sleep,
starched doilies appear on the armchairs.
Every day's a chore.
Monday, errands. Tuesday, laundry.
Wednesday, bake lemon squares
for the knitting club luncheon.
Friday morning, clip coupons.
Put the pouch in your purse,
with the list, organized by aisle:
bananas, 3 ripe, 2 not so ripe
stew meat (on sale), onions, parsnips
Chicken of the Sea (5 cans), Dutch noodles,
Listerine (coupon expiring), 3 Kleenex.
For a treat, *2 boxes of nonpareils* to last the week.
That night, you slide the chocolates out
from under silk and lace,
re-read the yellowed letter.

Self-Portrait

I have a history of quitting.
It started at Miss Dolan's Dance Studio.
I failed *shuffle-ball-change*,
developed a Shirley Temple phobia,
then quit piano after I botched
"Traffic Cop" at the recital.
I like long walks in old cemeteries.
In a drizzle of grace, stones vibrate.
I prefer winter to spring, its absence of songbirds.
Human nature's my fascination.
I'm repelled by frogs, bees, snakes;
wonder if phlox is a disease
or a breed of deadly spider.
Even the forests oppress me.
I'm fond of cobblestone-clotted streets,
but love the music of wind and water.
I'd choose fog over sun.
I crave dreamless sleep
when the Ferris wheel of vision-thought stops.
I think too much anyway.
It took me years to read again, after the injury.
I wish I could love again.
I'd start with the planet; try to recycle.

Bribe

I quit school at seven.
Sister Barbara Ann, too young to be so mean,

put me in the coat closet
for mispronouncing VERY.

Never saw a V and a Y together,
learned a Y could be VERY tricky.

The next girl up to read
stumbled over the VERY same VERY.

Sister blamed it on me—her mistake.
Mine—correcting her:

Grabbed by my Peter Pan collar,
shoved in with the coats until lunchtime.

Even now, I remember being very relieved,
more comfort in that closet than classroom.

At supper, I announced I was through with school.
By bedtime, I told the grown-ups why.

They let me stay home, not even punished—
for being fresh to Sister.

The next day   and the next,
I wouldn't go to school.

My parents panicked.
So they bribed me

with the *Bride Doll*,
all that I desired.

I beat that doll,
knocking her veiled head off.

Mea Culpa

I wasn't kind
to Eileen Keneally

mea culpa

unkempt and shy, her sin—
abject poverty

dishwater hair, painfully thin
"cooties" the taunt would begin

picked-at scabs covered her limbs
"on the count of three leper and run"

I wasn't kind
to Eileen Keneally

mea culpa

ragamuffin wraith
silent haunted eyes

never dared to cry
whipped and scorned as He

on her way to Calvary
and I as scared as she

of childhood cruelty
I wasn't kind

to Eileen Keneally
mea maxima culpa

A Brief Stint as a Nurse's Aide at Sunnyside Manor

I hated the undressing
lifting the dead weight
swinging the legs
lowering her into the water
too hot, no — too cold!
So I began to run the bath
all hot, to watch her flinch,
control the berating.

Those scaly feet
those cottage cheese legs
and droopy breasts,
the smell of yeast rising.
Quick swab of the folds below.
Shampoo the gold-gray hair,
hear the yell — *my eyes!*

So I began to forget the extra towel,
one to sit on, one to dry her.
I'd leave — breathe,
come back when she was shivering.
Lift, dry, powder, dress her.

That Sunday, I slid into her room
to take the lunch tray and found her crying.
Mother's Day — no cards, no visitors —
I turned away.

Zero Newbury Street

I met Judy Garland
right before she died
on Christmas Eve.
Barely sixteen,
my first real job—

Spotlights bounced
off mirrored shelves,
high-heeled shoes
and pointy-toed boots,
not meant for comfort
or warmth or human feet.
Glittery.   Dangerous.
Wear me and men will want you.

She came in near closing time
in full length mink
that couldn't keep at bay
the bite of holiday lonely.
Bright red lipstick, spots of rouge,
gobs of black mascara
highlighted her haunted glassy eyes,
wide with the dread of barely living.

How I wanted to protect her—

Those vultures on commission,
vying to try to make her buy
those not-quite-ruby slippers,
whose tap-tap-tap of heels
and magic incantation
failed to ever whisk her home.

The Angelus

He always came home at 6
until the day he didn't.
I was ten. JFK was shot.
Dad took shots of vodka.
Listerine covered it,
or butter rum lifesavers.

He hid it in the laundry basket;
stuffed it in the ash barrel,
or in the glove box.
Drove the wrong way
up the expressway
on Labor Day.

Carol told on him.
Mary thought *I* told on him.
How could I tell? I didn't know.
Even when he fell in the street
on the way home.

I was supposed to believe, so I believed…

He went to daily Mass,
confessed Saturday afternoons.
She talked to the priest.
"No divorce unless he hits you."

His boss called her in,
"No more sick days."
She left with his pay in her purse.

I gave up on God.
My horns started showing.
Every night at 6,
the church bells ring—*the Angelus*—
Behold the handmaiden of the Lord...
I want to pray. I can't pray.
His blood was wine.
His body bread.

I was supposed to believe, so I believed...

The Telling

One by one,
the eldest first,
summoned
to the dining room.

They come back up,
red-eyed zombies.
More gray silence.
I'm the last to go.

Raindrops trickle down
the bay windows.
In a straight-backed chair,
she's dry-eyed:

"No sense breaking bad news at night.
Your father—unexpected."
I feel the bitter, brimming,
see her face melt like a cheap candle.

My childhood ends—
I reach out, stitch her back
into starched control.
Her cheek—smooth stone.

The room chills—
and cobwebs quiver.
I hear him whisper:
Be good to Mother.

First Binge

Mrs. Shea brought over Butterscotch Blondies
after Daddy's wake—

gooey, brown sugary,
caramel and butterscotch chips

not the Nestle bits
I was used to.

But I wasn't used to
neighbors in the parlor either.

In the dimly lit pantry,
I cut sweetness into dainty squares,

arranged them on the Blue Willow cake plate,
two dozen, two-inch treats—

I tried one—so soft and sticky,
the taste I associate with fresh grief.

Carol makes the tea. Mary is serving the ginger ale.
I stay behind the pantry door.

I eat every last one.

Blessed Sacrament

The casket's now closed —
inside, someone who used to be
my father. At the wake, neighbors
murmur, "He looks good."
No he looks dead.
My father is not dead. That is not
my father.

The priest chanting
Et lux perpetua luceat eis
while swinging the censer;
then the casket passes
down the aisle.
Incense and carnations,
the cloying smells of sorrow.

My mother follows it,
the boys holding her up,
one on each side;
the girls walk together
clinging, sobbing, loud.

I hold my uncle's hand;
see my ten-year-old not-quite-self
float up and out the stained glass dove,
its gold streams of light, cold.
He is not here. I am not here.
We're not bodies. We're air.

The choir looking down, staring at
the me-not-walking-down-this-aisle.
A tear begins to fall.
I swallow this salt.
I won't let you go.
I won't ever cry.

After the Funeral

(for Mary, at thirteen, on Father's Day)

You had made the sprinkler bottle
at Scouts for Mother's Day,
spray-painted a Coke bottle pea green
and curled yellow ribbons to its neck.

Now you fill it with cold water, and take
each white cotton button-down shirt,
two weeks' worth, out of the laundry basket;
sprinkle the collar, sleeves, back, right and left front,
roll them up and place them in the refrigerator drawer
after removing the iceberg lettuce.

Cold shirts, sprayed with starch, hit by heavy iron,
until twelve ghosts of him hang
from the plate rail in the dining room.

The smell of him reunites—
The tang of his weary and worried heart
rises from the sweat of that button-down job
that killed him. He was the only one
who understood you.

Mother drags herself home,
from the 7 – 3 shift
to find him resurrected.
So she stuffs each perfectly ironed shirt
into a garbage bag.

That was the last time
you tried to be good.

Fifty Years Gone

Is he with my brother now
or in my son's marrow?

Or in the blue mist of dawn
rising over Spot Pond?

Is he under the umbrella at Nantasket
working the crossword puzzle?

Does he see me playing Bridge,
finally finessing the Queen?

Is he in the bleachers at Fenway,
hand over heart, singing the National Anthem?

Or playing piano at the Footlight Club—
"In the Still of the Night?"

And is his heart broken by the Church's disgrace—
better a millstone…drowned…?

Or in the V of Canada geese,
their bereft notes of departure?

And is he the spark and smoke
of autumn leaves, burning?

stone

Snug Harbor

a meager sun
in steel blue sky

the bitter wind
off ice-clogged shores

the surf submerged
silenced

*You listen to what's said
and what's not said*

how they teach
about suicide

a herring gull
its wings tucked in

clam shells smashed
like a burglar

You listen to what's said

its yellow eyes stare
then I hear

"thanks for trying"
that frigid edge

the doorknob truth
before leaving...

On-Call in the ER

He rose from the orange plastic chair,
handsome still at eighty.
A skyscraper in tweed, he gazed down on me
to hear news of Mrs. Stone.

From my slight sideways shake,
he knew what he already *knew*.

Grief calves a glacier.
Shoulders slumped, chin tucked to hide
his ice-skimmed eyes.
"May I see her?"

I went ahead down the dingy hall,
flickering with fluorescents, past the gurneys,
the mothers screaming,

to the last cubicle, curtained—dark, quiet
when some instinct signaled:
        "Wait here a minute."

So I saw the violence of cardiac arrest
how they opened her chest,
the cherry red stain still spreading.
I cleaned and covered her quick,
slipped out so he could say goodbye.

The ER's a cacophony again
as we walk toward triage.
In harsh blue light I knew —
his spirit had joined her.

I say what I'm supposed to say:
    "Is there anyone I can call?"

"No. No one."

Betrayals

The procedure, intrusive
as paparazzi, should be done
in the right eye, not the wrong one.

The third new trash barrel should
be left at the bottom of the driveway,
not thrown into traffic for roadkill.

The paint chip, *crocus*, should make
the clapboards look like the flower,
not the purple of a circus.

The tenants should pay their rent
or leave the place
as they found it.

The phlebotomist
should hit the vein
by the third try.

Jericho Road

Living on a dangerous curve,
I heard the distant thud
before eerie silence. Then
a tapping on my kitchen door.

The bleeding man,
arm at odd angle,
gash above right eye,
is on the other side
of the glass.
Inside me, all the weight
of all alone.

Lead him, drop
by deep red drop,
to my beige couch,
wrap his arm, bone out,
in a clean dish towel,
look into his blue eyes—
one pupil larger—ask:
"Is there anyone I should call?"

"My mother.
Saw your light on."

The Police come, check
his Jeep for dope, finally
call the ambulance.
Flashing lights pierce midnight—
he's my responsibility, no longer.

Yet, I am haunted by his stain I sit on.
If he were drunk, mean, armed—
would he have bled any differently?

Edges

In a black shallow bowl,
three lemons—brilliant
in morning light,
as the tea steeps brown,
the serrated knife slices
one thin perfect circle,
its juice flows onto the cutting board,
into the day's bitterness.

*

A letter opener slits
the official letter—
foreclosure. Handcuffing
herself to the porch rail,
she readies the shotgun
as the auctioneer arrives.

*

That weak ankle snaps
on the icy stairs—
grab the handrail.
Car keys slide
in with the trash
and eyeglasses appear
in the icebox.

*

A pencil-point sun
traces green through gray,
until the approaching squall
erases light.

Beebe Woods

First you notice the absence
of civilized sound.
Time seems shut off,
beneath your haste, a quiet holy.
Each step, an amen.
Pine and oak intertwined,
birds back early.
Suddenly a chill—
there is no Here.
You're in a long ago lost—
in summer, a lake, tall pines,
twisted paths, thick with needles.
This way? That? Hours pass
walking, crying, walking, getting dark...
There may be no way out.

Omen

If one night were my life,
or a single minute,
this would be it—

Faint drizzle on the shoulders
of your black raincoat,
like tears of relief from winter.

We walk down cobblestone streets
under those acorn lamps' glow; it bends
rose-gold off brick and bay windows.

In each window box on Joy Street,
deep blue-and-yellow-faced pansies
long to merge, to spill over.

Out of warm March mist appears the number 76.
You open the shiny door, shake the damp off our coats.
We follow the maitre d' to the back corner table.

Then the candle flame
flicks the hurricane globe,
it explodes—

Lament

Must you spew
that whiskey litany
and rub smooth
those barbed slights
into ice night after night
and snap those shame
pangs into kindling
and must you wear
your bones outside
that starched shirt
to document your
fractures and save
all your green grievances
to throw into the fire
that just smokes
but can't catch—
like your minnow dreams.

That dream of you again

this time—a deranged pope,
rushing from pew to pew
in a holy rage to save,
touching the heads
of the kneeling children
as each one leans to kiss
the heavy holy ring;
your cataract blue eyes glow.

But now you're one of the entourage,
the brown-haired curate,
carrying a camera,
you move in shadow,
from pillar to pillar,
following the Holy Father,
capturing the upturned
faces of young boys.

Later, alone in the darkroom,
those faces float into view,
like when he touched you,
taught you to find that relief,
an unholy loneliness
before satiated release.

Willie Nelson, 4 a.m.

It was autumn, that first frost
    when you left without a fuss,
slithering out one day with courtesy.
    "Here's where to send the mail."

Was it too much effort for you
    to give me a real goodbye or
    have a satisfying fight?
Instead, you left me kindly—the cruelest way.

Left me to rake the leaves alone
    put away the patio furniture
    stock up on firewood
and fix the storm window you broke
    last spring—all the small abandonments.

And while I was waiting to hear
    "I love you" or
"I'm sorry, I didn't mean
    to get involved so soon."
All you said was
    "Keep the CDs and the drill."

You even left your favorite shirt—
the black and green check flannel
    with the tear in the elbow
that I never got around to mending. The one
    I sleep in now.
The one I always said made you look
like Harrison Ford and you knew then

you were my very own superhero,
   my very handy man.

...little things I should have said and done
   but I never took the time.

Now there's an early storm
   and I lie awake listening
for the sound of you tracking in wet, fresh snow
all over the linoleum.
   This time, I wouldn't mind your leaving
that jacket on the kitchen chair.

Palimpsest

(on finding a poem tucked in the back of Cavafy's
Collected Poems at Tim's Used Bookstore, Provincetown)

Who tried to expunge his pain,
writing out Cavafy's "Come Back"

in longhand three times? These poems
musty now—ink, a faded gray,

the loops and curls intertwine—
each a stroke of foreplay.

Below the third copy, new verse
tight cursive in sharp red ink—

At last, instead, lips, skin and hands move as if unbidden.

Like the pain trees know—violent
wind that wrenches limbs.

The ending, hard to decipher,
these rushed, red words—

Yet another meeting in the present dark,
a rising, to be kissed...

At the Red Inn, Provincetown

Maybe it's just the way
women weather storms.

The wind whips her rainbow umbrella
inside-out and the sea grass sideways

as though it, too, could run
in from the gale.

Inside, it's nearly empty—
the quiet of the hour before dinner.

We shake off the damp of the day,
the intensity of listening.

Settle in with a carafe of red wine,
begin knotting the threads of affection.

"Did you notice how the men talked over the women?"
"And how the women let them."

So easy, trained to be docile, to follow…
Then words spill fast as rain, coursing down the windows.

Laughter, an occasional wave
washes up and over the patio.

We gaze out at sea and sky blending
its gray-white-violet light,

no longer sure where one begins
and the other ends.

Trashpicker, Orchard Street

(after Naomi Shihab Nye)

Rounding the corner
from the back of the house
in early evening,
watering can in hand,
I startle her. She startles me.
Who belongs here?

Her amber eyes hold my gaze.
I look away. She could be me.
She's not old or young, almost pretty.
Trim and neat, smooth black hair
pulled into a bun, she bends and mines
my recycling bin.

A beer bottle drops
into her plastic bag, clanging
with the shame of wastefulness.
She walks west down Orchard,
smiling her hoarder smile.

Iris

(from: "Life on the Line, the People of Bus 19" by Billy Baker,
Boston Sunday Globe, July 17, 2011)

Iris worked three jobs—days, nights, weekends.
One, the meat packing plant in Norwood. Slipped
while butchering pork. Stairs slick with fat. Fell,

crushed her knees. Surgeries. Doctors' bills
suck up all she saved. "Workers Comp don't cover living."
So she keeps the freezer fully stocked, every cabinet topped off.

Up and out by 6. Empty cart. Ticking clock.
Her workday now, 10 hour slogs, long waits in weather,
food pantry to food pantry.

Bus 19 heaves along Geneva Ave., hisses to her stop, Twelfth Baptist.
Eighth in line. "Eight is good. Rice, beans, juice for sure,
with luck, creamed corn and chicken gizzards."

At nearly 7, it begins to drizzle. A three-hour wait till it opens.
Back on the bus that spits her out at Seventh Day Adventist. Iris among
the desperate—pushing: *Primera vez. Primera vez.* First time. First time.

Food and fear, fear and food, cart and clock, next stop.

Mind's Eye

(*La Gitana*, Louis Kronberg, Isabella Stewart Gardner Museum)

Not the gardenia-painted comb
in the crown of her slick black hair
nor the curves of her shawl, its rosebuds
swirling like Spanish dancers,
not even the little curl defining her cheekbone,
but how her hand frames her face,
its fingers pressed against pursed lips,
thumb tucked in under her chin
as if to lock in the unspeakable.
Her amber eyes express such liquid sorrow;
her lids, lower slightly, sharpen
her gaze. A cold knowing
settles into her marrow, into mine.

Nightmares

                    Arriving late
at the first tea dance
of the season,
ice blue chiffon and tulle,
making your way through
the sea of teeth—
even your best friend's
smirking. Now everyone turns—
the dress unraveling.
Piano legs revealed
in garter belt and nylons.

                    And *that* one again,
after a day of aggravation,
scurrying through
a brick-lined alley,
you spot steep cement steps—
run—the train's coming!
Its screech of brakes,
its rising steam, white-blue,
the sudden shove—you're falling…

                    You're trying to fly:
Where to go? Even the rocks are unraveling.
Now images from the past flash
in grainy footage—men in lead suits
shovel debris back into the reactor.

          But now you're him—
one of the leaden, the blond one,
with stone eyes, brimming,
showing pictures of Tatiana at two,
leukemia. And then you try again,

little Vladimir, just a baby.
Two sets of blue eyes, eternally staring.

Before Dreaming

She curled into a question mark
        of not quite sleep, wondering
what becomes of wrongs and slights
        as sharp as cheddar
without the sweet apple of "sorry."

Do they become that lobster dream,
        you know the one—
where you get lost, take the wrong exit
        off the bridge, get stuck in traffic
behind the perpetual construction project,
        leave the car in frustration,
forget your shoes and purse,
        get yelled at by the female cop
for abandoning the teddy bear in the back seat,
        then walk through all those lobsters
        pinching at your feet.

She knows what her therapist would say:
        "You are everything and everyone in your dream."
Lot of help that is!
        "He's the lobster, not me," she always complains.
That nitpicking nitwit sleeping so soundly
        it's annoying,
lying like the exclamation point of righteousness,
        remembering none of his dreams.

Maybe we are different species—
a collie and an ostrich,
not meant to mate,
          or just two porcupines shivering,
quills of protection no comfort at all—
                    her last foggy thought...

If I wake up dead…

call the undertaker 1-800-GOT-BODY
turn the heat down to 60
air out the bedroom
empty the refrigerator
take the trash out Wednesday morning
mail the bills all made out
lavender sweater, at the dry cleaners
spare cash in the sock drawer
forward the mail to Purgatory, Canto XX
change the outgoing message: Alice doesn't live anymore
close my eyes, coins in bedside table—
on top of obituary

Death of Teaticket Hardware

I never knew his name,
nor he mine.
He was always there.
Patient. Polite. Shy.

I never knew the name of what I needed, either.
But he did. After listening.
"You know that thingamajig
that connects the hose to the washer."
"I need the innards of a lamp."

He'd find it in a flash—
through overcrowded aisles,
so narrow only a munchkin could maneuver.
In the back of the store, on the dusty top shelf
where whatsits live.

He'd tell me how to use it.
And he'd tell me again,
drawing it on the little scratch pad
he kept at the register (not the electric kind)
next to the dish of pennies
and the bowl of lollipops.
I would always leave with a red one,
        and confidence.

He was the kindest man in town.

I imagined he went home at 5:30 every night
to the apartment above the store,
and told his wife over meatloaf and mashed potatoes
green beans and pecan pie:
"That lady came in again today, seems bright enough
but doesn't even know a lamp has a socket."
And he'd smile when she would say, "Oh, Mrs. Dimwit."
And they would turn on the News at Six.

The drive to town is eerie now
that Teaticket Hardware is gone.
Boarded up windows stare like a zombie
whose soul's been stolen by Wal-Mart.

Peter Cabral, son of John, son of Peter, son of John,
I never said hello, or goodbye, or thank you.

marsh

Praiseworthy

Consider how horny the bear
that swam the canal and ambled
down to Provincetown.
Praise the search for a mate.

I'd like him as a date—
stroke his thick fur coat,
let him keep me warm.
I'd tongue his honey-pot,
be his Goldilocks. Keep
his sleep-kissing secrets.

So, he's not faithful?
I'd trim his claws back
just a little,
let him toss his hard
ranger hat on that chair—
too soft anyway.
Even let him smoke
his pipe in bed
after his tooth-marks
have dotted my thighs.

Praise the roaming.
Praise the searching.
Praise the quickie.

Praise Reverie

Forget the excuses—*no time, too busy.*
Let cyberspace evaporate.
Silence the cell. Don't call the office either.
Ignore the urge to be needed.
Pretend the cheddar growing mold
is the discovery of penicillin.
Don't think of the starving children.
Don't think of anyone.
Splurge.
Paint your toenails *Thrill of Brazil.*
Sit still and let them dry.
Allow the wind to lift thought away
and the sun to lull you.
Inhale salt air. Breathe out light—
see it slice the crest of waves.
Become the illuminating green
and the flash in foam.
Dip those ruby toes into cool water.
Feel luxury surge
from toe to head to toe.

Meditation in the Garden

English ivy's new green leaves poke through the splintered bench
    and swirl up the gnarled apple's trunk. A bee
        enters a violet bell, pauses, ceases to buzz—

I see myself swinging from that limb jutting out, falling doo-dah down.
    I was eight then.
        Where has most of my life gone?

A tiny red spider spins the first thread, works with purpose, intent,
    an architect of the complex. Would Robert Frost be proud?
        I close my notebook now.

Dew-etched in the breeze, the spider, a bridegroom awaiting his bride.
    Don't sit under the apple tree with anyone else but me...
        Why am I hearing this song?

No sign of spider. No trace of web.
    Quick as that—both disappeared.

Diva

Lit from within—
each soft cream
petal unfurling
with a little
delicate curl
at the tip
like whipped meringue
a stillness suggesting motion
their sweet, smooth fullness
revealing erect gold threads
no wonder the bees
are rubbing and buzzing
like Ella doing Cole.

Snug Cottage

In garden shade, dew disappears,
bees enter the violet bells
of sun-drenched hostas,
a cabbage moth floats by, dips
a u-turn, its wings—white silence;
as the fountain trickles,
a pair of finches land
splash, drink, bathe,
flit their brilliance away;
people begin biking by,
brrringing, breaking the spell;
I turn to look back,
my cheek brushing the moth
that rests for a moment on my shoulder
as if to say: *You're not alone.*

daylily

if you watch
or not   it can't stop

what is now   will not be   ever again
unless

you hoard it
polish it up   in the white of winter

when the worst   and the best
of cold   keeps you locked

in ice-gray
then   let this brightest light

unlock   your deepest dark
even if brilliance   fades

O summer's gold strumpet
what does it cost   to bloom for a day

morning air

swept in the screen door
in the moist salt of summer

waking me like a lover
kissing the rounded me

its flickering tongue like the waves
upon the sand   insistent

then fingers fill me
I'm the moon tide   overflowing

boneless   floating
in the moist salt of summer

I merge with morning

Harbinger

(after James Wright)

All the windows are up.
In flies a catbird's scratchy call
and crisp apple air.
Late August light is chiffon and shimmer—
its nights, a fine chilled wine.
Savor the last sip. Shut the poet's book,
The Branch Will Not Break.
But the leaves are starting to fall.
The rooster will still crow at dawn.
A jet plane's white plume is dissipating
high above the marsh.
Most of my life has flown by.

Labor Day

Smell of endings
decay of day
evaporated time of summer.

Should we count
our lives, not in years
but summers

or count the Scrabble score
with made-up words—
piggygate and *wuzies*?

A yellow shovel carried off
by late day surf,
the sandcastle leveled.

Tide of taillights ebbing
as last cars cross over
the Bourne Bridge.

Shadow Darner

Early September, on the hem of evening,
in light that sparkles before it dims,

I sit on the blue glider,
absorbing the language of light, studying its silence.

Then a dragonfly lands next to my hand
and for an hour keeps me company.

O! You—with your ebony head,
red cowl-neck and slender body.

Each of your silver mesh wings
has an identical dab of rouge.

In a sudden shift of air, you disappear.
Across the bog, a few leaves fire off a flare.

Autumnal Equinox

One night the empty glider
rocks, fretting.
Next day—a sweater.

When does dimmer light
turn green to khaki
and cooler air court
yellowing of leaves?

The sun dips
earlier and earlier
into Buzzards Bay.

Evening ribbons
streaked pure pink,
deepening to purple.

Night erases its own canvas.

Snapshots of Sippewissett Marsh

I. Late Afternoon, Labor Day

a lone swimmer parts
    a pewter sea

a cormorant on the rocks
    wings apart, drying off

a large, speckled gull flies off with a Birkenstock,
drops it against a rock, like a clam shell

thunderclouds churn
the surf's froth to meringue

a dad, "the tide's going out."
    his son, "is it because it's tired?"

undeterred, like the dominant bird,
the dad's preoccupied with packing up

II. Light, Early October

Nothing gray remains—
days of rain and fog dissolve.
Now the sky's bleached blue,
with a milk skim of clouds.
Shafts of light pierce tips of red-gold grass
and spear the lapping shore
till every stone and shell begs to be held.

The water's warmth, seductive,
toe by toe in for one last dip—
Eros' salty shiver.

III. An Early Turning

We used to say "that one's sick,"
that maple, across the marsh,
but somehow I think it smart,
prepared for the hunkering down—
the first to sport a copper crown,
before the extra blanket,
and the furnace turned on,
before the faithless flocks depart.

Indian Summer
(after Charles Wright)

Again and again, morning light
bathes the marsh and saturates
its green with gold.

Life, held in abeyance,
does not move on or back,
back or on.

Each day like the last.
There is no next,
at least not now.

Wetlands in June

Twilight flicks each new leaf
etched gold on green
that guards this frog and insect Eden.

Calls of birds   shrill   sweet
every   squawk   trill   honk   peep
lingers like fireworks in the beyond of dark.

Time as still as oak and pine,
who can divine is this the first night of summer
or the last of spring?

Darkness deepens to quiet.

The child I am (and always was)
sees brilliant yellow finches fly
inside my mind:

a night light to depend on.

Wetlands in October

This swamp earns its keep in autumn.

Flame-tipped leaves spread,
like thighs under a lover's touch,
    across a still body

where every undistinguished bush
and bramble burns, furnace-red pure
    of the dross of existence.

    Now, the light loves my marsh
more than spring's lacy-green
    or summer's lush underbrush.

Now, leaves swirl and dip,
    dancing red—the tango.

Life darts from bush to vine
        to heaven.

Wetlands in November

(for Terry Burke)

Oak leaves cling despite
the biting storm, so now I see
the beauty of browns: rich
like old leather-bound books.

And the sole Fairy Rose,
tinged with pink, survives
its vibrant neighbors.

Why are the subtle ones strong
and the brilliant ones gone?

Then the wind quickens
and scrub pines sway,
till the tallest one snaps—
first blackout.

My last match lights
my only candle.

Cape Cod Fog

Rain falls on old snow.
Gray gauze wraps
edge of land and sea,
as cool air settles
over warmer water—
the road home a ribbon,
tying night to nothing.
No up. No down.
No way out.

Bourne Bridge

Not the hard rain
the rivers crave,
not the downpour
to quench the forest floor,
just a light mist,
on almost empty roads,
as I'm entombed in gray,
the only sound
an intermittent shush—
wipers clearing windshield;
this quiet is pleasing,
a monochromatic alone,
when suddenly the overcast
lightens from charcoal to dove,
then splits into strands
of mauve, salmon, rose,
and the bridge ahead, luminous,
wrapped in a pale blue shawl,
each raindrop clings,
glistening in pure light
that's always there
even when hidden—
I've come home.

About the Author

Using humor and memory to celebrate people and place, Alice Kociemba is the author of the chapbook *Death of Teaticket Hardware*, the title poem of which won an International Merit Award from the *Atlanta Review*. Her poems have also appeared in *Avocet, Cape Cod Poetry Review, Comstock Review, International Psychoanalysis, Main Street Rag, Off the Coast, Plainsongs, Roanoke Review, Salamander, Slant,* and *The Write Place at the Write Time,* and in the anthology *Like a Girl: Perspectives on Feminine Identity.* She was a featured poet in the Spring/Summer 2015 issue of the *Aurorean*.

Alice is the founding director of the Calliope Poetry Series (www.calliopepoetryseries.com) at the West Falmouth Library, and since 2009 has facilitated a monthly Poetry Discussion Group at the Falmouth Public Library. She has also served as the Guest Editor of Volume III of the *Cape Cod Poetry Review* and the 2015 & 2016 editions of *Common Threads*, the poetry discussion project of Mass Poetry. She is the first poet to receive a Literacy Award from the Cape Cod Council of the International Reading Association for promoting literacy through poetry.

When asked, "How did you get interested in poetry?" Alice credits Emily Dickinson with saving her sanity after she suffered a severe head injury in 1986 and couldn't read, drive or work for six months. Shortly thereafter, Alice wrote her first poem, "seizure," about her experience.

Born and raised in Jamaica Plain, a neighborhood of Boston, Alice now works as a psychotherapist in Falmouth, MA, where she lives in a house overlooking wetlands.

CPSIA information can be obtained at www.ICGtesting.com
Printed in the USA
BVOW08s1100180216

437166BV00002B/6/P